Poems
and •
Stories
from the Heart

Poems

and

Stories

from the Heart

Peter Knoester

Kravitz & Sons

INNOVATORS IN PUBLISHING, MARKETING AND ADVERTISING

Kravitz and Sons LLC
204 E Arlington Blvd. Suite B
Greenville, NC 27858

Published by Kravitz and Sons LLC.

ISBN: 979-8-89639-461-7 (sc)
ISBN: 979-8-89639-460-0 (e)

Library of Congress Control Number: 2026902319

Table of Contents

The Mighty Oak

Oh mighty oak, thou hast been slain.
Thou hast succumbed to wind and rain.
A mighty wind, it howled and blew.
The power of which, thou never knew.

No birds again will nest in thee,
For now, thou art, a fallen tree.
Thy branches were high in the sky,
But now on muddy ground they lie.

Thy leaves will soon wither away,
They will not see another day.
Thou shall be missed, by all who see,
But most by me, as I loved thee.

Finding Love

Where has my heart wandered off to?
It has gone into this unknown world,
The sights I see are alien and strange.
I try to touch that unreachable but can't.
What is it that beckons me to go further,
To go deeper and deeper into that great abyss,
Where all thoughts are stored and where memories
From so long ago are buried and forgotten?
I shiver to think what I may dig up there.
Where is the part where love is stored?
Oh, there it is, it is a large box and when I
Opened it, it says, "love of self " and it startles me.
Am I like that, no really, it must be a mistake,
I loved a lot of people and now this?
Get me out of here and let me think about this
For a while, as surely I know what love is,
Or have I had it wrong all these many years?
Turning inward I experience a strange feeling
Of inadequacy, of having been left behind,
While others expressed their love so freely,
And I holding back that essential part of life
That gives meaning to everything around me.
I see it now as I stand back and look at myself,
I am suddenly overpowered by a force that opens
The eyes of my blind heart and now, love rushes in

And goes into every crevasse of my being and I
Become like, what others have always been,
Alive again for ever more, with love to spare.

Tormented Heart

When I look back on the times gone by
And feel the emotions again of the past,
I wonder whatever possessed me to wander
On the path that led me to this sorry state.
I know that to see me you hardly do notice
The aches that so torment my heart for so long
But go on I must as time does some healing,
Although ever so slowly, as memories last.
Who knows what the future will bring to us all.
The hopes and the fears, whatever befall us.
What is it that plays on our mind and our soul
To keep us going in this circle again and again?
I know they all say, don't live in the past,
Look forward and enter a new way of life,
Which will make you happy and not sad.
It is easy to say, for those not in my shoes.
At ease with myself I must become,
On the gentle waves of my thoughts,
And the blue skies that hover over my soul
Trying to dispel the gathering clouds of fear.
Religion creeps in and gives me thoughts to wonder,
What path to take, instead of laying down in slumber.
Wake up I must as time goes by so speedily.
Get hold of the truth, which always sets one free.

I wrote this down to speak to myself and wonder
What is inside of me and to impart to others,
That, no one is alone and no one is an island
No matter what, it's only love that can cure all.

Serenity

As I walk on the beach of my home town at the water's edge, I look back and see my footprints in the sand. It's like looking into the past as I see my trail fading in the distance. The thoughts I had then have already been forgotten. I follow my trail to where I am now and seem to go from the past back into the present. I can hear the waves softly lapping against the shore and the seagulls are flying high aloft soaring on the gentle breeze. Their cries may be directed at me for coming into their world or maybe just at each other, I don't know. In the distance, I can see a ship slowly passing across the horizon, it seems to be standing still but of course it isn't. My shoes are crunching the sea-shells that are lying on the beach but my eyes are not on them as I do not care because my eyes are not on them but on the surroundings that I am in, on this early morning hour. There is no one around and the serenity revives my soul and all unpleasantness falls away as my eyes take in the vast expanse of sky and horizon. I try to become one with it all, to also float away upon this gentle breeze to be carried to places as yet unseen. Try as I may I am earthbound and I pity myself for not being able to do this. As I am getting close to the ramp where people come on the beach, I see some coming now. For a while I thought this beach to be mine and that these people are intruding on it. I hate to share this moment, but they have just as much right as I have. I turn around and start retracing my steps and with it I disappear into the past to get back to the present.

The Fall

The fall has come with all its grandeur,
And all the leaves will show their splendour.
There is no other time my dear,
That can compare this time of year.
It's really nice but also sad,
As soon enough the leaves be dead.
Then they will fall upon the ground,
Where all the other leaves abound.
Which is too bad as now you'll see,
The trunk and limbs of a naked tree.

It is I

Behold a man, who is not wise.
He's lying down, but will he rise.
The morning comes, he thinks too soon,
So he decides to sleep till noon.
The hours come and waste away,
And so it goes most every day,
When will this man wake up and see,
That he who's lying there, is me.

What My Heart Feels

What is the word to describe a feeling so deep,
That it fills all the pores of my being?
I want to reach out and touch the ones I love,
Without them knowing that I do so
Because I don't want to reveal my feelings.
What a foolish notion that is and how naïve,
As what else is there which expresses one's inner feelings
Than the very action of embracing and caressing
Those you love and care for in your life?
Oh take away this hesitation, and let me let out a yell
So loud it can be heard around the world.
A yell that comes from feelings so long held in,
That now burst forth with such force, that it breaks
Open the heart that has so long been silent and suffered
So long, because of the absence of love in one's life,
The raging flood of love that overwhelms me so
And pours forth to those who were so close to me.
Still holding back a little as we are too scared to
Let anyone see the hurt and pain endured for such a long
time. I see these words and know their meaning, but will the
ones Reading this, understand what goes on inside of me?
Day after day, do they see the loneliness which abound in
me, Which causes this expression in words on paper?
Who will read my plight and who will sympathize?

Only those who are in the same shoes and seek an outlet
Through words spoken from the heart and mind
Of a tortured soul, silent for too long and now overflowing
With love, knowledge and understanding.
We look up from the bottom of this pit of life,
And look up for the rope let down so that we who see the
light,
Will climb out to the light and embrace the fact that there is
A sun, and we will bask in this sunlight and forget that which
Has been and look forward to the day that we can embrace
Our loved ones without shame of showing our true feelings.
What sweetness, what love and care that day will bring,
To be whole again and united with all you loved and love.

Beyond Our View

Beyond our view there lies a land where dreams are born.
It's there I wander and languish, in that lost domain,
Where there is neither strife nor sordid language heard.
I love to linger in that place, to have my soul restored,
And fall away into that forgetfulness and ease the pain
within.
To touch that perfect world is my goal and what I long for.
Oh how I hate to go back to the real world so called,
For who will understand and who will take my hand.
And lead me back to that place where peace is king,
And reality far away from the dreams that I dream.
However I must go back into that realm that's called reality,
And remain again a while and bide my time until
Again, I will enter into that place that I love so much.

Thoughts in Flight

When thoughts are in flight and look down
over the barren fields of nothingness,
Wanting to reach out and bring life
where there is just mental dust.
How it aches and tries to influence
that part that is dying for lack of will.
Oh let there be a miracle which causes
that which is dead to come alive,
And breathe in again that life force
that seems to be forgotten so long ago.
How could something so sacred
have been forgotten and put away
Into that part of the mind where there are so
many reminders of life within?
Please utter the words which will be
the evidence that not all is lost,
And emerge from the dark side of the mind
to again be the power of old.
Rejuvenate the mind and let the soul hear
the music of the harp, softly played
And be satisfied with that old saying,
that spring is indeed hope eternal.

A Mother's Love

Behave yourself my mother said,
Or I will send you to your bed.
I better heed my mother's words,
Before she will be out of sorts.
I love my mom and she loves me,
That's plain for everyone to see.
She hugs me close when I am cold.
'Cause after all, I am four years old.

Persevere

Our dreams will sometimes turn to dust,
However going on we must,
To build new dreams that will last longer.
Adversity will make us stronger.
Don't hang your head and pine away.
Tomorrow is a brand new day.

Business Opportunity

A plum, a plum, I see a plum.
I grab hold with finger and thumb.
Oh boy, oh boy, it's now I see,
I got hold of a bumble bee.

Near and Far

Even though I am far away.
I think of home most every day.
Of things I did and didn't do.
The happy times, the sad times too.
I know the past I cannot alter,
The more I try, the more I falter.
What's done is done, it seems to me.
Change what you can, the rest, let be.

Abide

It's yonder hill that beckons me,
From there it is, that I can see,
That other world, that's not my own
But alien to all I've known.
My world, it is not built with stone.
But just a farm where I have grown,
And learned to live a simple life.
A world that is not full of strife.
So here it is, I will abide,
And not cross to the other side,
Where cities thrive and have their ways.
My home I love, no other place.

The Meadow

As I am walking along my road on this early Sunday morning, I come to a misty meadow where half a dozen cows and their calves are grazing. They look at me with big, opaque eyes that are like deep pools of black water. It does not take the calves long to get used to me staring at them, as they realize that I mean them no harm. Soon they are darting around on stiff legs to express the life force that is within them. I almost burst out in laughter to see them frolic like that, but I dare not as it would be like disturbing the peace. Some flies are flitting about and seek out the fresh cow dung. A bumble bee hums right around my head, startling me, as they have been known to sting people, I leave him alone. High aloft are a few wispy clouds heralding the coming of another beautiful day. I smell the dew on the grass, and the early morning light bounces and gleams off anything that is wet. The glare is hard on my eyes, but I love it so, as the world around me seems to be made of gold and silver. The night moths have settled down, and the butterflies are already busy pollinating the road side flowers and weeds. The morning mist is now rising as the sun gains its strength and evaporates the moisture from the plants and grasses, all too soon in my opinion, but we must all abide by the rules and laws of nature.

A sudden strong breeze whips through the quiet meadow, picks up the vapours, and drive them into the trees surrounding the meadow. Everything is seen very clear now. All too soon, all too soon, my heart says, but I know that nothing lasts forever, as time moves on with unstoppable force and even this fine Sunday morning must come to an end.

Life

The heart of the matter is not what we think of life,
But of what is in that life we like to think is ours.
Are we at ease with what we have accomplished?
Or is there another urge which drives us onwards?
We are born, we grow in understanding and knowledge,
And a course is set towards what we call, destiny.
All the waves that life brings with it, we survived,
But all leave a residue that shapes our character.
Were we praised growing up or used and abused?
Or were we born with an abnormality or illness,
Which prevents us from becoming what we wanted to be?
Do our parents' genes play a part in all of this?
Is destiny like a scroll which unrolls until we die?
Can we not deviate from it and is fate all we have?
Oh how we wrestle with this, as how can this be?
The happiness of parents to have a child born to them,
And then watch the child become something other
Than what they had in mind for him or her.
To perhaps become a Hitler a Stalin an Attila or murderer
What are their thoughts, "wish he or she was never born"?
To these things there is no end and all talk is useless
Like a rock thrown in the pond the circles ever widening,
Engulfing everything and affecting the whole pond.
So it is with a person and his actions, it effects his circle.
Like a word spoken in haste it cannot be unspoken.
Or like a bullet fired, it has its own destiny, for good or bad.
I can see that there is nothing else than that we enjoy life,

And give happiness to all those around us, lest we stray.
We must walk the path that so many did before we started
ours, And be one with mankind, the universe, this earth, this
life